BANNER-M TO THE

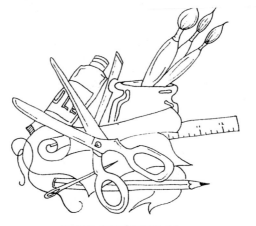

BY ROYAL

APPOINTMENT TO THE KING OF KINGS

Edited & compiled by
PRISCILLA NUNNERLEY
Line drawings by Jane Garrud

CHRISTIAN BANNERS
Amersham

By the same author:
An Army with Banners
First published 1982
Reprinted 1984, 1986, 1988

Banners in His Name
First published 1986
Reprinted 1988

ISBN 0 9509307 2 5

If you want to base your banner on a design from
the Good News Bible as a matter of courtesy you should first
write to the Project Co-ordination Manager, Bible Society,
Stonehill Green, Westlea, Swindon SN5 7DG
for permission as they hold the copyright.
In most cases permission will readily be given.

Designed and Printed in England by
Nuprint Limited, 30b Station Road, Harpenden, Herts AL5 4SE.

Banner-Makers To The King

Acknowledgements

My grateful thanks to all who have shared in this book.

To my parents for their love and support.

To my sister Rosas Mitchell for her enthusiasm and constant encouragement.

To Stuart and Christine Reid for their friendship and example and to Stuart for his input into my life of 13 years preaching.

To Roy Pullen, my other pastor, for sharing with me in the struggle and excitement of this book.

To Ruth Wood for her steadfast friendship which has kept me pressing on and for all her help with these books.

To Angela Duff-White and Terry and Elisabeth Pearce for their relaxed and happy hospitality.

To Gill Douglas, of St Michael-le-Belfry, York, friend, collaborator and inspirer.

To Jane Garrud for her skilful and imaginative line drawings.

To Clare Ashburner for contributing so much of herself and her creativity.

To Gill Peters for her cheerful support and for typing the script.

To Trevor Bruton for excellent photography.

To Margaret Mason for her encouragement and for checking and improving the manuscript so skilfully.

To Doris Sayer, our church secretary for her kindness and help.

To my church for all their interest and prayer.

To Renee, Megan, Liz, Myra and Philippa of the 1988 banner group for their sense of humour and fantastic support.

To my housegroup with its happy and stimulating leadership by Jim and Pauline Dudley.

To Rodney Shepherd and all at Nuprint Ltd for appreciating the purpose of these books and for printing them so attractively.

Finally, to the gentle leading and guiding of the Holy Spirit in every aspect of editing this book.

This book is written by people who acknowledge Jesus as Saviour, Lord and King. We see the banners as an expression of our love for Him and the making of them as a high calling. We believe that we are called and appointed to the task in the same way as those who make music for worship.

A key verse for me as editor has been, 'My grace is sufficient for you for my power is made perfect in weakness'. This book is written on my part from a position of weakness rather than strength. Such a place leads to dependency on the Lord. It is an opportunity to prove His power and the glory goes to Him.

In lifting up the Name of Jesus and His word we are giving Him honour and proclaiming His triumph over Satan and so it is inevitable that spiritual warfare is part of the process. But we ride under the banner (the word means victory) of Jehovah Sabaoth and the Risen Christ and victory belongs to Him.

Thank-you so very much to all of you who have prayed this book into being and especially to the friends in the 1988 banner group in Amersham. Banner-making is about people. It is a delight to be together with others; the love will remain when the banners are tattered remnants!

Some of us came together while this book was in the making and this is our statement giving freedom of copyright. 'We see our creativity as a gift from God to be shared with others. Although it is good to have fresh inspiration for each banner, it is impossible to be entirely original and so you are welcome to use some of these ideas and techniques in making your own. We strongly recommend you don't limit yourself by copying complete banners because you will miss the creative process of prayer, meditation and design which is at the heart of banner-making for the Lord.'

Living Banners

Roy Pullen, The King's Church, Amersham, Bucks.

This book is about the good news of Jesus Christ, the Son of God and Saviour of the world. It will show you something of the great variety of ways used by the Holy Spirit to make the gospel come alive for us. Through words and pictures the excellence of the grace of God is proclaimed in giant exclamation marks.

The editor and contributors to this book on banners would like to share with you, the reader, the richness of God's revelation of Himself and His ways to them, together with the means through which He has inspired them to share that revelation with the wider church family through the creation of many different types of banner. Essentially, these folk are not merely producers of fine art work, but they are men and women in whom the Holy Spirit has moved to bring the Word of God to life. This is what banner making is about—proclaiming that we have come face to face with the living Word of God. The words and pictures convey what has been born in the hearts and what is being worked out in the lives of those who cut out and stitch and sew and paint and draw to produce a living statement that affirms and proclaims the Word of Truth.

Of first importance, then, for any who want to become involved in banner making, is that they should have a living faith; a personal trust in the Lord Jesus which is marked by a life-style that confirms and expresses faith. In the fertile ground of your living faith the Holy Spirit will speak to you—about words and pictures, colours and shapes, textile and texture. He will speak to you in panoramic pictures and He will lead you through the minutest detail, as you ask Him

The words of Mary
to the servants at the
wedding at Cana

with faith for the word He wants to bring to life for you and for your brothers and sisters in the church. My own experience as a pastor is that often the banner group comes up with a banner that is complementary to the theme that is being taught in the church, and many times they have started work on a project long before that theme has been settled upon by the leadership. God is very good at 'working all things together for good'.

By definition, a banner bears witness to the presence of a leader, of a king. It is a focal point, a rallying point that invites people to acclaim the king. It is a meeting point that says, 'Here you will find the king.' It is a flag lifted high so that those in the heat of battle will take courage; so that the hard-pressed will not give up; so that the weary will be re-invigorated; so that the satisfied will not settle and the victorious will not cease from going from victory to victory.

We are communicators, not primarily of feelings or pleasing ideas, but of the eternal Word of God. The psalmist declares: '...you have exalted above all things Your Name and Your Word.' And of the Word of God, A. W. Tozer wrote: 'The Scriptures are in print what Christ is in person. The inspired Word is like a faithful portrait of Christ.' Banners—are a powerful way of presenting that Word, the truth of God and one of the many tools of the Holy Spirit.

Editor's Preface

Creativity often comes out of difficulty and pain. Times of depression have been my springboard into colour, design, and a riot of materials. They have given me a new awareness of the visual world around me. Out of the wintry ground spring the daffodils. Out of the darkness of a camera comes the colour photograph.

In making banners and communicating the banner ministry the Lord has given me fresh skills and taken me beyond my natural capabilities. As I have stepped out in faith and been prepared to work hard the Lord has supplied the gifts and ability but I have had to learn to spell the word 'faith', 'R I S K'. The Lord has taken the initiative in giving us His word and the presence of His Holy Spirit but we have to step out in faith to obey what we believe He is saying. We have only one life to risk in His cause!

Creativity comes most of all from spending time just being with the Lord, through talking and listening to Him each day. Ideas for banners have not fallen from the sky! They have come out of my friendship with the Lord. I have places in my spirit like a sheltered garden by the sea where I walk with Him. I sometimes neglect this priority of making time just to be with Jesus. I need to realise that He longs for my company much more than the manufacture of endless banners!

A dream of *An Army with Banners* (printed in 1982) seeing the people of God move out into the streets and market place, is being fulfilled in these days. Banners are the flags of a people on the move and we are proclaiming the love of Jesus and expressing our desire to bless and serve and see salvation, righteousness, peace and justice come in our land.

A continual challenge to me, over the years that these books have been written, is the statement of Jesus, 'And this gospel of the Kingdom will be preached in the whole world as a testimony to all nations and then the end will come.' Brother Andrew said about these words at Mission '80 at Lausanne. 'Only as we take the Good News to all nations will the world be ready for Jesus to return.' I see banners as just a small part of bringing in the Kingdom and preparing the way for His Second Coming.

JESUS TURNS YOUR

This side in shades of grey

This side in full colour

DARKNESS INTO LIGHT

A Set Of Banners For A Modern Church

Trish Aze, St Andrews, Hatters Lane, High Wycombe

Three and a half years ago, our church was in the throes of building a large extension, with a new worship area. About six months before its completion, I looked into the building and saw that there were three windows down one side and two on the other. In between the windows was a blank wall facing diagonally into the church. These blank spaces immediately seemed to cry out for banners! Very quickly the covenant names of the Jehovah God came strongly to me. My father had preached on these names when I was a child and I had never forgotten them. Shortly after, I came across a leaflet with about ten names written down, complete with references. The name Jehovah seemed to me to refer to the God of the Old Testament. There is a majesty, power and mystery about it that we rarely think about today.

Firstly, I went to our vicar and discussed with him the idea of a set of Jehovah banners. He was very enthusiastic and gave the go ahead. Next, a notice was put into the church bulletin for anyone interested in banner making to get in touch with me. Five ladies came forward and we started our group. Previously I had made single banners on my own, usually, as and when I was prompted by the Holy Spirit, so leading a group was a new experience for me.

At our first meeting we prayed together, discussed the implications of the name, Jehovah and looked up the references. Jehovah is God's personal name: 'My name is JEHOVAH' (Ex 6:3). God used this name when he wished to make a special revelation about Himself concerning His moral and spiritual attributes. In Exodus 6:6 God spoke to

Moses and called Himself 'I AM'. Jehovah (I AM) comes from the Hebrew word HAVAH 'to be' and sounds like the Hebrew name YAHWEH, traditionally transliterated as JEHOVAH. This name is represented in many Bibles by 'the LORD' in capital letters. It speaks of God's faithfulness and unchangeableness, and also has a continuous tense implying a continuing revelation of God to men. When Jesus said, 'Before Abraham was, I AM', He was claiming to be equal with GOD. In fact, all the Jehovah titles find their fulfilment in Jesus.

We decided together which names we would use for a set of six banners—five for the walls and one for the front. We decided to have a large size (size 74" x 54") to cover most of the space. With a set of banners, the choice of harmonising colours is extremely important. We took one name at a

time and thought about it silently, then pooled our thoughts about the background colour. We found ourselves in agreement with five of them and the sixth colour was chosen to blend in with the other colours, and, in fact, turned out to be very suitable for the banner's title. Two ladies went to a big store and chose the colours by taking the rolls of material and putting them side by side, mixing and matching until a harmonising set was chosen. The emphasis was on colour rather than the type of material and they bought curtaining materials (four of one type and two of another).

The colours were:

blue for Jehovah Shalom—the LORD our peace, reminding us of blue sky, light and peace;

brown for Jehovah Rapha—the LORD our healer, representing the Cloak of Jesus the hem of which the woman touched to be healed;

green for Jehovah Jireh—the LORD our provider, representing the green earth and growing things, reminding us of God's abundant provision;

red for Jehovah M'Kaddesh—the LORD who makes us holy, representing the cleansing blood of Jesus who died to make us holy;

dark orange for Jehovah Sabaoth—the LORD of Hosts, representing a glowing fiery sky;

gold for Jehovah Shammah—the LORD is here, speaking of the glory of God.

Working on the designs required a lot of hard work and prayer: By what I would call direct revelation, one lady had the design for the Jireh banner and another the design for the Rapha banner. Jehovah Shalom easily came out of discussion and Jehovah Shammah came out of an earlier vision given at the church about our new building. Jehovah M'Kaddesh was a combination of ideas that we felt were incorporated in the meaning of the name. The Jehovah Sabaoth design was more difficult, though we knew that we wanted an angel. One lady wanted an angel with wings, while others wanted a stronger image. Finally, the description of God's armies in Revelation 19:14 inspired the angel-soldier riding on a horse and blowing a trumpet.

The main Jehovah titles were all done in the same style of lettering to give unity. The English wording for four banners was made using ribbon or tape and the words, 'The LORD is here', on the central banner used the background colours of all the other banners. The banners were paired, in that the blue background had brown letters and the brown background had blue letters. Similarly the orange and gold went together and the green and red together.

As with all banner-making there was inspiration, prayer and much hard work, but through it all there was a sense of the Holy Spirit's presence, guiding and helping us and bringing excitement and expectancy. Many times we were not able to meet altogether as a group, as two were nurses on shift work and others had different commitments, but two or three would come to my house in an afternoon and we worked together in such a way that each person concentrated more on one particular banner than another. One person did all the main lettering and another the English words, yet in the end it felt as if the whole set was our corporate work. The responsibility for the banners was a very big one. The church building was new and beautiful and the banners therefore needed to be of a high standard to match but, above all, they needed to proclaim to all the majesty of God and the power of His Name.

They were well received and caused much comment. A booklet explaining the banners was given out, and a series of sermons preached on the titles depicted. The set stayed up for two years, till a new set depicting the I AM's spoken by Jesus in John's gospel replaced them using bright background colours and a different shape and style.

No Condemnation

Carol Clarke, Holy Trinity Church, Knaphill, Woking.

The idea for this banner came from Rhoda Hazeldon, a member of our church dance group and I asked her to share how she was given the picture. She said: 'The song that inspired the banner was

> God has a garden and He calls it praise,
> And He bids us to enter, to walk through the maze,
> Well it's like an ocean so vast and so free,
> And God said He made it for you and for me.

> And in that garden there's freedom from sin,
> There's no condemnation to those who walk in,
> Because of the keeper there's love all around,
> There's healing and blessing on His glory ground.

I am in the church dance group and we were at the time preparing to dance to this song.'

The main points that made the picture clear in my mind were complete security: a wall around the sides, but a never-ending garden with always room for more; rich colours worn by the people dancing signifying the richness of God's love, and the joy and happiness shown by the dancing; birds denoting freedom, and flowers and trees belonging to God's creation.

'No Condemnation' seemed an apt title. The archway denotes the personal relationship with God; every person that enters is individually cleansed and released from guilt. This banner has proved a blessing to people in our congregation and I hope will continue to be so.

We needed to make this banner quickly to have it ready for the dance the group were working on. We therefore decided to use only material we already had. This decision

Holy Trinity Church,
Knaphill, Woking

presented certain problems in that the main piece of blue material upon which all the details were to be stitched was rather limp, so that we therefore tried to use heavier materials for trees and the wall to give it the necessary weight.

We wanted the banner to be very bright and colourful, with the grass 'spring-green' but we had nothing suitable. We worked around this problem by using yellow overlaid with deep green net. We chose felt for the many flowers to make it easy to secure them with one or two stitches (usually, we herringbone stitch every piece of material to prevent any fraying and, if a dark cotton is used on a light background, it can enhance a shape by giving a distinct edge).

The wall and arch were padded and brickwork stem-stitched with wool to create the rough effect. The dancers all carry a tambourine and here we were able to add sequins to represent the 'jingly bits', and little ribbons fastened at one end only to add to the 3-dimensional effect.

We make it a point always to include at least one sequin on each of our banners and enjoy finding the best place to add one or more. They always catch the light when the banner is hanging. (One thing we have learned—always use a cupped sequin rather than a flat one which can look like a black spot in certain lights).

We did not worry about perspective in this banner— the woman in the archway should be much bigger—but concentrated on placing figures, including children, to create a scene of joy and freedom.

Have you noticed one of the figures is wearing a bright purple gown with gold sash? One person, on seeing the banner for the first time, commented: 'I'm glad to see the Bishop is there'!

The banner has a permanent place on our church wall and one older member of the congregation sat beside it for weeks before suddenly realising the truth of the message in it. Needless to say she was jubilant.

Pastors, Paper And Pasta

Liz Rutty, The King's Church, Amersham

This slightly off-beat title refers to several influences which have proved important to us in Amersham during the past year or so as we have sought to continue exalting the Lord in making banners.

Pastors

One of the main projects we have undertaken recently has been a large material banner constructed in four separate sections but designed to show one whole picture. The idea for this particular banner first came at an informal meeting the banner group had with one of our pastors, Roy Pullen, when we invited him to come and chat with us about his feelings concerning the group's ministry. He suggested that Proverbs 3:5–6 would be a challenging and apposite verse for the church.

> Trust in the Lord with all your heart
> and lean not on your own understanding
> in all your ways acknowledge Him
> and He will make your paths straight.

Using these words we decided to make two banners to hang as a pair—partly for the practical reason that a great many letters were involved. The first part of the verse was simply done with letters on a plain material background with a 'frame' of patterned edging.

However, for the second part of the verse, Megan had an idea for a striking design of mountains, valleys and streams to be executed in the four panels to form an integrated whole. We have often been surprised and thrilled when appropriate materials are found to enhance the banners we are making and on this particular occasion an old seventies era skirt was donated to form the basis of the four

panels we needed. Renee used some gorgeous, eye-catching, shiny fabric in deep mauve for the mountains and Myra had fun constructing some hand knitted sheep.

There were practical problems in making a complete design in four separate panels. Particular care had to be taken to ensure that the design flowed accurately across the panels and that the letters were put on straight! However, it was very easy to take away parts of the banner to complete at home. It took us about two months to finish this project.

Paper

During the past year we have made a number of paper card banners. The first four paper banners were to illustrate a series of sermons on the theme 'New Life in Christ'. That theme was suggested to us by the pastors but the actual verses or words were chosen by ourselves. The four phrases we selected were:

Set free (Jn 8:36).

Perfect love drives out fear (1 Jn 4:18).

From one degree of glory into another (2 Cor 3:18).

Therefore if anyone is in Christ he is a new creation (2 Cor 5:17).

Paper banners may be relatively simple and quick to execute but the theme and design need to be thought out as carefully as any other kind of banner. However, the 'Set Free' banner shows how effective just a few pieces of card can be, in this case black, orange and gold. At first we wondered whether to give the figure a Biblical-style robe and appearance but decided to make it a more twentieth century figure, which gives a surprisingly dramatic sense of the Truth that Jesus does, indeed, set us free.

Our most recent Christmas banner was also made of paper and card. Speed was of the essence here as we had about three weeks only to complete it. Priscilla, our leader, started the ball rolling by asking us to read out verses about Christ's nativity and coming into the world. We then had a time of quiet and meditation considering the truth of the words we'd just read. At the end of this time, I felt very

strongly that the words from Matthew 1:23 'Emmanuel— God with us', were right.

We decided to make a collage based on the main street in Old Amersham with its lovely old buildings. We took photographs and from this drew an outline of the shapes of the buildings and these were cut out in grey card. The windows, doors and features were drawn on and then cut out and backed from behind with shiny paper in silver, gold, red and blue. This banner was displayed during the Christmas period when the theme 'Emmanuel—God with us' was reflected in music, song and drama during the services.

Pasta

Well, you might be wondering where does pasta come into all this? No, we haven't yet entered the realms of design using swirly shapes of macaroni and tagliatelle, feasible though this proposition might be! But we have enjoyed working together, praying together and relaxing together— at most of our meetings there's a great deal of laughter, fun and enjoyment. So on many occasions we've had meals together—sometimes quite simple meals, sometimes more elaborate such as at Christmas time when we invited members from two other local banner groups to join us and get to know one another better.

These occasions have symbolised the love we have for each other, the enjoyment we have in each other's company and the joy we've all experienced in this particular way of serving the Lord and proclaiming the Truth of His words.

My beloved SON

by Mary Davis, Blandford Evangelical Church, Dorset

I came into banner making through a keen interest in sewing, particularly in patchwork and quilting. Having tried a number of traditional patterns I branched out into designing my own fabric pictures mainly of friends' houses, landscapes and seascapes. My mind was continually being opened to new ideas with unusual fabrics and this awakening, combined with a renewed and growing faith, came to a climax when I saw, for the first time, banners hanging in a Church. I had such a strong urge to produce my own inspirational hangings that using my self-taught skills of needlework and, perhaps, a natural sense of colour and design, I embarked upon the first of many banners which now hang in Churches and homes.

The vision for the banners comes through many channels but the source is always from God. I can be inspired by a number of things, whether it be the spoken word, verses from the Bible, a situation, a celebration or just the everyday beauty surrounding all of us, if only we will stop a moment to appreciate it.

The purpose of the banner is to share with other people the same vision and experience that I have received from God. Some of the banners I have made speak directly into a situation and allow the viewer to simply ponder on such thoughts, while other banners are less obvious and the interpretation is more open, the observer being able to feel and interpret an experience in his/her own particular way.

In retrospect I realise that my banners rely much on colour and contrast of fabrics, perhaps not so surprising, considering that it was my pleasure in fabrics that first brought me into banner making. Shape and design also play an important role and this is probably the area I find most difficult as here I have no formal training. The two banners, 'My Beloved Son' and 'A New Creation' illustrated in this book, show one of the techniques I have used in my banner making.

'My Beloved Son'

This banner is 6' x 3'6" and was initially made to publicise the musical, 'My beloved Son', by James Davis. From a purely practical point of view it needed to be bold, to be understood immediately, and to leave the viewer in no doubt at all as to what he or she was about to witness. It also needed to be a design which could easily be reproduced in a one colour print for publicity.

The inspiration for this banner came from Matthew 3:16–17 (AV). This is the focal point in the musical and the title words also come from these verses.

> And Jesus, when He was baptized went up straightaway out of the water. And lo, the heavens were opened unto Him, and He saw the Spirit of God descending like a dove, and lighting

upon Him; And a voice from heaven saying, 'this is My beloved Son, in whom I am well pleased.'

I felt I wanted to depict the power of the Holy Spirit together with the voice of God. This strong feeling of power coming down is represented by the descending doves coming to rest on the baptismal waters. This power was so strong in my mind that it dominated the whole scene and I felt that to show the figure of Jesus would have weakened the design. Instead, I used the rather strong swirling lettering of the title on which to rest one's eyes. I 'felt' the design for this banner. I did not sit down with pencil and ruler and try to work out geometrically how I could illustrate the 'power' or the 'voice'. I could almost physically feel the weight and hear the sound and so the design flowed quite naturally.

The central dove has such strength and movement in its swooping position and yet if you close in on just that one dove it has a real look of delicacy and innocence with its soft blue sequined eye and pearlised feathers. The silver threads from each wing woven through the net background help to centralise the doves as if they come from one place and this triangular effect is reflected in the water.

The suggestion of the shimmering water needed to be no larger than it is. Its shape not only reciprocates the shape of the descending doves but adds depth to the design and illuminates the place where Jesus stood. From a practical point of view the sequined material would have been too heavy (and too expensive) to cover the lower half of the banner.

In the initial stages the title lettering was neatened and given a 'style' for me by a professional graphic artist. It is very bold writing and has a real flair about it. Consequently I chose white satin bias to help facilitate this flow and appliqued it by hand onto the net.

The background is formed by many layers of blue and turquoise net. The layers were individually hand sewn to a white cotton backing so that I was able to get this graduation in colour from sea to sky without an obvious horizon. To obtain the effect of distance the doves were appliqued under different layers of net. The central dove is padded, quilted, embellished with beads and sequins and appliqued on top of all layers. Tassels hang from the top at either side.

The banner can be mounted on its independent stand and has been used by Churches not only to publicise the musical but also to illustrate other themes such as baptism, the Holy Spirit and the life of Christ.

Behold the beauty of the Lord
Psalm 27:4

Banners And Dance

Jane Wyatt, the King's Church, Chesham

El Shaddai

When I heard the song I fell in love with it. 'El Shaddai' means God Almighty. My flatmate, Sally, and I thought it would be good to do something together: Sally would dance and another friend, Rosemary, and I would make the banner and we would get someone to sing with the backing of our music group.

The banner shows the difference between Mary's grief at the foot of the cross and her joy when Jesus rose from the dead three days later and her realisation that He would be with her always.

This is what the colours signify:
grey, the past
yellow, promise and hope
blue, the eternal unchangeable nature of the Son of God.

The red on cross and figure represent the shed blood of Jesus. The dancer dressed in the same way as the figure in the banner.

Perazim

A banner, a dance, song and sermon were all linked to this theme for a morning service. 'Perazim' was the name of a battle site of David's victory over the Philistines and it means, 'Lord of the breakthrough', (1 Chron 14).

David himself also experienced the Lord breaking through into his life when he faced up to his adultery with Bathsheba and repented. Psalm 51 expressed his words of sorrow and repentance. The Lord forgave him and used him mightily in days to come. This psalm has been preserved by God for generations and to bring immeasurable blessing— to many people.

The dance was based on the words, 'Lord of the break-through' and the words of Psalm 51 and showed a struggle between five black figures and one white. Black represented sin and individual problems that were a barrier between the white figure and the Lord. The white figure represented forgiveness received in answer to the prayer, 'wash me and I shall be whiter than snow'.

The banner showed a figure, dancing from shades of black coming through greys (done with net) to a white figure in a position of tremendous joy and release. The message that came across is that whatever your need/problem, your personal Perazim, God can break through.

A Conversation with Rosemary and Jane

How do you meet together?

We tried to form a banner group but this never took off. People didn't want another night out. Recently, two of us have met as friends and ideas for banners have grown spontaneously. Jane has often taken the initiative in starting the design and we have involved other people in the sewing. God is a God of variety and I think our getting together can have a varied pattern too.

How do you get such beautiful finished effects?

We attempt to do the very best we can. I don't feel it would be right to short-change God on gifts he's given me; God has taken my natural talent and added to it. Give Him what you have and He will bless it and increase it. I enjoy working and seeing something come into being. I think there's a lovely place for doing things quickly—but generally our own projects take more time. When I'm working on banners I find myself very close to God. In doing something for someone you love very much you lovingly spend time.

Can you comment on colour?

When I see the way God works with colour I realise He must be a wonderful artist. Look at the way He made birds—

feathers—long-tailed tits with pink, white and beige—I feel He went around painting things and thinking, 'What can we do to make this one a different shape?' He delighted in creating different shapes and colours. He did it for pleasure. I, too, get a lot of pleasure seeing colours together. I like using the many hues and tones of colour.

Finally, brothers, whatever is true, whatever is noble, whatever is right, whatever is pure, whatever is lovely, whatever is admirable—if anything is excellent or praiseworthy—think about such things.

Philippians 4:8

Men Can Be Involved

*John Ward, Worple Road Evangelical Church,
Wimbledon*

It just happens that I am an architect, interested in design and graphics. I really enjoy designing things of any sort, and banners and visual displays provide a good opportunity.

Very often an artist, craftsman, or designer of some sort may well enjoy extending his skills to other media than the one in which he is trained. We need to explore more widely and thoroughly within our fellowships so that we can discover these hidden skills.

However, an architect is particularly concerned with structure, materials, strength, and support, etc. The assembly of a banner and its hanging is sometimes regarded as a secondary issue but is, actually, very important. Many men in our churches who enjoy the D.I.Y. activity in their own homes, could well be employed in providing vital practical help in such areas.

As an architect, I am very aware that banners, or any display, need to be seen in the context of their ultimate surroundings and church buildings should be designed with banners in mind. Wherever new church buildings are envisaged, or existing buildings are being altered, part of the brief for the architect or interior designer should be the inclusion and possibility of banners and displays.

There are various ways of providing adequately and inconspicuously flexible means of support for banners, such as well located hooks, continuous battens, or eyelets screwed into a timber ceiling to allow suspension by means of nylon cord.

*A working drawing of a banner made by
John and others in his fellowship.*

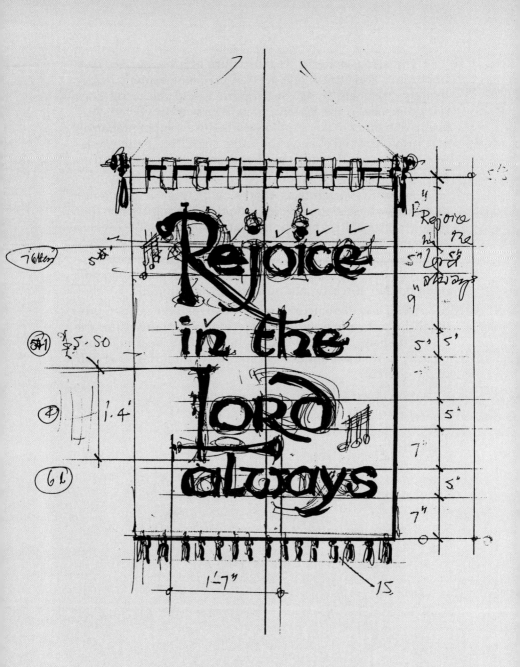

The actual material and structure of a banner are very important. Sometimes one sees an excellent banner, inadequately stretched, hung, or supported, and the result does not do justice to the amount of skill or work involved. Any group of banner makers could well involve men in preparing and providing the suspension rods, stretching battens, tassels, etc., even if they may not feel that they can contribute to the actual design.

As well as architects there are graphic and interior designers whose skills should be tapped. An impression that is generally held is that banners are made of cloth, involve stitching, and embroidery, and, therefore, are a woman's domain. With the advent of many forms of adhesive, the materials used in banners have widened considerably, and often neither stitching nor needlework is required.

Once an adequate method of suspension has been provided in a church building, there will be opportunities for visual displays on hardboard panels, notice boards or pin boards, as well as banners. So, start recruiting the other half of the church!

Banners For Processions

Rosas Mitchell, Murray Place Baptist Church,
Stirling, Scotland

Marches or processions have become a prominent feature of today's church as the Lord has called us to come out from behind our church walls and unite with other Christians in our towns and cities to proclaim Jesus.

Our banners are a vital part of this proclamation and will be seen from a distance and possibly on television or in the press. This means the banners need to be:

Bold

- They must be simple and clear. Small decorations will not show up.

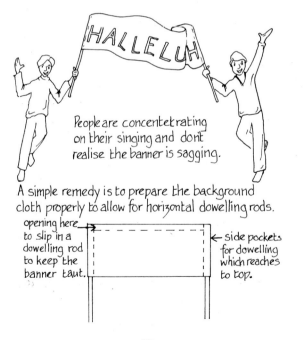

People are concentetrating on their singing and don't realise the banner is sagging.

A simple remedy is to prepare the background cloth properly to allow for horizontal dowelling rods.

opening here → to slip in a dowelling rod to keep the banner taut.

← side pockets for dowelling which reaches to top.

- There must be some large banners possibly 6–8 ft wide so that 2 or 3 people can walk between the poles. These very large ones should be interspersed throughout the procession.
- The letters must be very clear and carefully cut. Careless letters give a shoddy appearance and are not worthy of the Lord. Lower case letters are easier to identify at a distance.

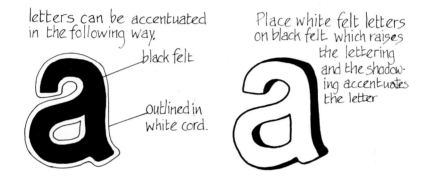

letters can be accentuated in the following way.

black felt

outlined in white cord.

Place white felt letters on black felt which raises the lettering and the shadowing accentuates the letter

- Contrasting colours give boldness and clarity eg: — white or yellow on black or orange on navy. Primary colours show up well. Good effects can be obtained with fluorescent paper. The meaning of colour in praise and worship can guide decisions.

Blue is the sky colour, the colour of the heavens. It can represent the infinite, eternal nature of the divine Son of God.

Green is the colour of growing things and speaks of life.

Yellow is the colour of promise, the future, heaven, joy and celebration.

Red represents the death of Christ, His sacrifice and atonement.

Purple is a royal colour.

Gold is symbolic of divine righteousness— kingship—majesty—joy and heaven.

Paste a sheet of fluorescent
paper onto hardboard.
Take a black sheet of
card the same size.
Cut out your words and
motif, and paste on top of
the fluorescent paper.

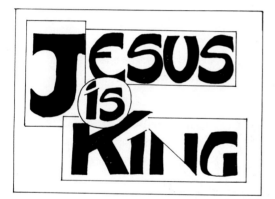

Stick coloured paper onto
hard board. Stick different
coloured shapes onto this
as a base for contrasting
letters of fabric or card.
Could be done in paint.

Dark background
rainbow coloured
balloons and white or
yellow letters. Cloth
paint or card.

- They must be prepared for adverse weather conditions. All types of banners can be sprayed with the appropriate fixer. If there is a strong wind, a few carefully cut holes will allow the air to flow through but it is worth waiting for the day and praying that it will be a still, dry one that will make these procedures unnecessary.

Meaningful

The words must be simple and their meaning apparent to the crowds who watch. They could be short words from the Bible or words taken from some of the Make Way Songs, for example, 'Shine, Jesus, Shine'. They can also be Biblical truths put in modern idiom. Think of incorporating these on banners indentifying your church or group.

Cover old umbrellas with cheap shiny material.

Make swivel sticks of cane or rolled up newspaper

Varied

Processions or marches need to display joy and humour, to provoke and surprise. Banners can be of all sizes. Hardboard placards can be made by taking a medium size piece of card and spraying it with a mottled effect. Then place a stencil on top and spray through it. Paste the card onto hardboard and nail both to a central stick.

Banners can be mass-produced in different colours in a very short time. Small banners can be made by children. Self-adhesive felt is a useful fabric. An adult can write the letters on the back, backwards, and the child can cut it out and paste it onto card which can then be stapled onto a small garden cane.

Balloons, swivel-sticks, and decorated umbrellas can all add to the fun. Felt doesn't stand up to rain so, if you want your banner to last, use other fabrics such as cotton or crimplene. PVC letters are very bright, waterproof and they do not fray.

Workshops For Processions

Prepare your pieces of fabric by machining all the seams. It is a good opportunity to get rid of unwanted gaudy pieces of material. Have a vast selection of fabrics and felts ready and also scissors, glue etc. Workshops can take place about six weeks before the event and then once more nearer the day. Or you may decide to do it all on the morning of the procession!

'Do You Love Me?'

John Harris, Emmanuel Church, Northwood

I *didn't even know* what the march was for. But I enjoy walking and it fitted the bill. Good stride, from North London to St Paul's, and as a new Christian, I knew I needed to 'go public'. Perfect! Quietly perfect!

I had the first hint of my error of judgement when we de-bussed in the park. There were several thousand people, and they were singing and chanting. Not to worry, they would probably quieten down when we reached more populated areas. But the banners. They made it clear what we were, and obviously they wouldn't be hidden as we marched—quite the contrary I feared.

Not to worry. I would engage my few friends in bright, animated conversation for the next five hours. If I ignore the outside world, it will ignore me.

We were passing through Maida Vale high street. It was a warm Sunday and 'the lads' had their pints on the pavement. How to get through unnoticed. Of course, the banners. There was one in our group. Large, held in a socket belt with a wooden batten top and bottom. It billowed as we passed side streets and the bearer had to brace himself against being carried away like a square-rigger on a broad reach. I would hide behind it.

Then a guest of wind swung the banner and the lower batten struck a young girl and hurt her. Partly to prevent its happening again and partly to help the bearer I steadied the banner by walking in front and holding the batten.

I passed that pub, then another, and another. Nobody jeered. I felt stronger, and better, and happier as I walked, helping to make sure the banner would be seen by all.

The next day (Monday) my boss asked me if I'd had a good weekend. He is very affable but not Christian.

'Well,' I replied 'it was different.'

'How so?,' he asked.

I took a deep breath. 'I walked through London carrying a banner saying "Do you love me?" '

He looked at me, astonished.

'And,' I said, 'I would do it again.'

A 'Make Way For Jesus' Procession

Jan Hoare and Margaret Wyatt,
The Church of the Holy Spirit, Bedgrove, Aylesbury

The visual side of 'Make-way' was stunning as a 1,000 plus people walked through Aylesbury, Bucks on a November Saturday 1988. How could people not turn their heads to look and wonder what it was all about? A young man who came to the Lord at 'Make-way' said the sight of all the banners really drew him. Although he could not remember the words on them he knew that something special was happening to him.

We held workshops before the 'Make-way' to encourage people to meet and carry banners and also use them in their churches and personally. The outcome of these workshops was much greater than we'd hoped; so many banners were made and used. We were so blessed by the contacts and new friendships with those in other churches.

Provocative Banners

Trish Aze

These are banners to disturb and challenge, to make Christians sit up and think and take action. They can be used powerfully in the right situation and often are needed only once. Sensitivity is required to know that God's message, not merely the views of an individual, is being expressed.

They can be used:

- For Good Friday to bring the message of the cross.
- For Christian Aid and TEAR fund days—Pictures to make people think about famine, or injustice. A photograph collage of Jesus for TEAR fund Sunday contained some challenging pictures of Christians in difficult circumstances.
- To remember those persecuted for their faith.
- In 'Make Way' Marches etc; perhaps a strong, provoking verse could be used together with proclaiming verses on other banners—such as, 'let justice roll down like water'.

The Spirit of the Lord is on me,
because he has anointed me
to preach good news to the poor.
He has sent me to proclaim freedom
for the prisoners
and recovery of sight for the blind,
to release the oppressed,
to proclaim the year of the Lord's
favour.

Luke 4:18–19

This paper poster was made to challenge us to give for New Testament's for Russia. It was only up once on the Sunday morning that we had a speaker from—'Open Doors.'

Starting A Banner Group

Gill Sathy, St Martins, Barnehurst, Kent

If you are thinking about starting a banner group you may feel you do not know just how to go about it or lack the courage to take the plunge. If you are in this state of mind, trust in the Lord, cast fear aside and go ahead.

All you need is enthusiasm and a desire to create something for God and his people—for God will help you to overcome any obstacles or difficulties that may face you.

For two years I had wanted to do something artistic. When the Christmas pictures that had adorned the pillars every previous year disappeared, when the vicar retired, I began to think of a venture that might replace them.

I went to a 'Banner Day' in March and was overwhelmed by the beauty of the banners I saw that day: some were very simple, some were very decorative, but they were all done with praying hands and for love of the Master. The day of fellowship and sharing fired me with an enthusiasm for banner making. On the way home in the train I started to design an Easter banner with the words 'Christ is Risen'. The first words I read in the church magazine were in bold print 'Christ is Risen. Alleluja!' This confirmed for me that these were the right words.

So I started making an Easter Banner on my own, realising that it may never be hung in my own church. At that time we were without a vicar, and obviously I did not know whether the new one would support the formation of a banner group. I worked away at the banner as hard as I could, sometimes asking my two boys and my husband for advice about the letters and design, and sometimes seeking help from my friends. Events overtook me. My Easter Banner is still not finished. It will be one day.

During that period from March to October, I spent a great deal of time in praying and thinking about the formation of a banner group and in searching the scriptures for texts which could be used on banners. Although sometimes I was very impatient to get started, it was an important time for me—learning to wait on the Lord, and to submit everything to Him in prayer.

Our new vicar, Jonathan, arrived in July, and he welcomed and encouraged the whole idea. I just thanked God for his support. The Church Council unanimously passed the motion that a banner group be formed.

I made a simple harvest banner on my own of oats against a red sun using fabric paints and pens, and learned a few more intricacies in banner-making in the process.

I was becoming a little bit apprehensive about the whole idea when, while chatting to Jonathan, he said, 'Remember, Gill, it's not your group but will be the church's banner group.' I don't know whether he thought I might boss the group about too much but I do know that the doubts and burdens of the preceding weeks were immediately lifted from me! I realised the success of this venture was not up to me or, indeed, any individual but would be up to the group and to God.

The idea of banner-making as an aid to worship was launched through a talk during the Sunday evening service. The next evening an introductory meeting was held and, much to my surprise, eleven people came. We had a lovely evening together. A friend gave us some handy tips and good ideas. I had prepared a list of twelve texts which could be used for Christmas banners. We briefly discussed these, and decided to make four banners, one being made by one of the Sunday Schools. Each person was given a copy of these twelve texts to take home and decide the four best and draw designs for them if they wished to.

The first meeting of St Martin's Banner Group took place the following week. We began our meeting with a short time of prayer and meditation to quieten our minds

and feel the presence of God. The whole meeting went off very smoothly and many important decisions were reached. We chose the four texts and four designs, the size of the banners, the banner background, the type and size of lettering. We decided to have one evening meeting and an afternoon meeting as there were too many of us to meet together all at once. It was only after I reached home that I realised that one design had been chosen from every one of the four people who brought along designs. My heart was full with praise and thanksgiving.

The words, which I had read out at the beginning of the meeting were from Exodus 23:20–21:

> See I am sending an angel ahead of you to guard you along the way and to bring you to a place I have prepared. Pay attention to him and listen to what he says!

These words were true for us that night and for all our other meetings. We listened to our Lord, and He has directed us in the paths we should walk.

Since we started the banner group, in October 1988, I have come to see myself not so much as the leader of the group, but as a co-ordinator—bringing people together, providing them with a stimulus in thought and providing them with the materials and tools to create.

There is a price to pay for starting a banner group. It does not just involve the group meetings. You need time for thought and prayer; time to prepare; time to buy; time to do sewing not completed in the meetings; time to get all the necessary equipment together before each meeting. Do not be afraid to take a few weeks off after the completion of a banner or series of banners. You—and your family—will need a rest from them—as sometimes you will find that the banners take over your life!!!! Starting and running a banner group does take a lot of time and effort. However, I am just grateful and happy that the Lord has given me this job to do.

A 3D effect with the bottom 60cm of fabric folded back upon itself and very stiff card inserted to form a shelf effect – garden netting with covered cardboard fish. by Katherine Keast.

A Visual Arts Group

Enid Abel, Christ Church, Stone

In February 1987 came a letter to our vicar, from the Executive Secretary for the National Evangelical Anglican Celebration, April 28th–May 2nd 1988: 'Greetings! Is Christ Church still brilliant at creating banners? Could some be made to go behind each speaker in our 30 or so workshops?...' The venue, Caister Holiday Camp, Norfolk. So began our year's exciting, busy, exhilarating and hard working adventure with the Lord.

We have always called ourselves a Visual Arts group because we have made a wide range of items over the years and not confined ourselves simply to banners. We have always had a number of men in the group as well as women. In 1987, the group had a total of five experienced people. An appeal brought responses from a number of people—Margaret was one of them. She saw it thus, 'All welcome, come and help, no experience required.' So she joined—nervous and apprehensive—but she got hooked. 'The atmosphere, the involvement, the friendship, the exciting challenge all contributed to the urge to remain involved.' Elizabeth saw it as a 'desperate' appeal—'no real skills needed apart from paper cutting, glueing, tracing and maybe a little painting.' So she joined. Jeanette was another. 'The times when we've thought we've been incapable but despite just joining to stick, cut and glue, we've found the capabilities to do far, far more. Throughout all the project, the sharing, fun, fellowship together gave us tremendous pleasure.' Kath who has made banners in the group from its inception in 1979, writes, 'His banner over me is love. God's love is felt in the group as each member is able to contribute as they are guided and everything and everyone is enveloped in the fellowship of God's love as well as the trust in each other to work together for the good of all.'

one of the N.E.A.C. Banners.

The Materials

The themes of NEAC 3 were four aspects of God: Caring, Saving, One and Just. We made the decision quite early in the project that we would work in sugar-paper, card, foil, tissue and wall paper materials.

So God gathered the group together which varied in numbers throughout the project, but a total of twenty-two people contributed in so many ways and the ages ranged from 16 to 70+. The lesson we all learned was that, if we contributed our 'widows mite', God blessed it beyond our imagining. So perhaps God may be calling you to do your part in His project in your church or fellowship. We would say from our NEAC experience—step out and trust Him and you will be blessed as well as surprised at what you can achieve with Him.

We realised that we must aim for simplicity of style; variety came through using the same designs in different sizes. God led us to realise that it was better to use a limited number of designs in the different locations, so that people would recognise them and identify with the themes of the Celebration.

The process

George writes, 'the whole process of banner making should perhaps be best described as banner building. This seems a more apt term with the first spark of inspiration forming the cornerstone for many building bricks to come, inspired by fellow members of the banner building team. Don't rigidly go down the road of development wearing blinkers, be ready for the Spirit to move and, in doing so, be moved yourself.'

Margaret writes, 'The whole project, in fact, seemed immense and such a challenge! I couldn't see the whole picture. It was too much to take in and I was amazed how the leaders of the Banner Group actually had the nerve to accept the responsibility of the project and meet the dead-line date. I, personally, just kept my sights on the task I was doing.'

This banner was made with 3 dimensional fabric flowers. *St Matthews, Oxford*

This London bus was made for a procession.
St Jude and St Paul, Mildmay Grove, North London

St Andrews,
Hatters Lane, High Wycombe
Bucks.

St Andrews,
Hatters Lane, High Wycombe
Bucks.

This patchwork banner was made to convey the truth that Jesus directs our paths.
Murray Place Baptist Church, Stirling, Scotland

Murray Place Baptist Church, Stirling, Scotland

Easter banners.
St Martins,
Barnehurst, Kent

The blood of Jesus
constantly cleanses us
from all sin.
Sheila Turner,
St Mary's,
Sileby, Leics.

Made by the 4 Brownie packs of
St Martins, Barnehurst, Kent
for Mothering Sunday

Children's pictures drawn with
fabric crayons are stuck onto this
playgroup banner.
*Chalfont St Giles Christian
Fellowship, Bucks*

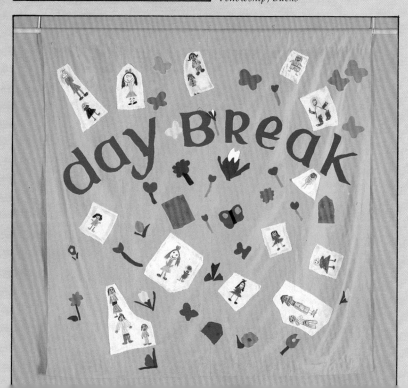

BE STILL
AND KNOW THAT
I AM GOD

A banner made from silks and satins with the reflection covered by net to give to desired effect.
Holy Trinity, Knaphill, Woking, Surrey

"Therefore if anyone is in Christ, he is a new creation the old has gone, the new has come"
2 Corinthians 5:17.
Mary Davis, Blandford Evangelical Church, Dorset

'And Jesus when He was baptised...saw the Spirit of God descending like a dove and lighting upon Him; and a voice from heaven saying "this is My beloved Son, in whom I am well pleased.'" Matthew 3:16, 17.
Mary Davis, Blandford Evangelical Church, Dorset

Biggin Hill Christian Fellowship, Kent

The King's Church, Amersham, Bucks

Cornton Baptist Church, Stirling, Scotland

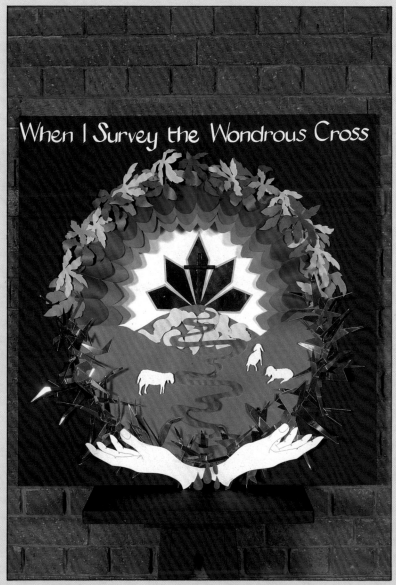

Our response to His love—the hymn 'When I survey the wondrous cross' portrayed in paper sculpture.
Pam Drew, Swan Bank Methodist Church, Stoke on Trent

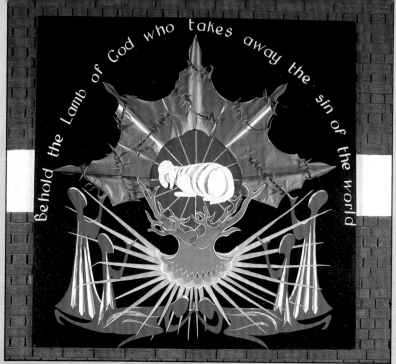

Behold the Lamb of God who takes away the sin of the world

Designed for Christmas, this paper sculpture anticipates the sacrificial death of the Christchild and His ultimate glorious destiny when He becomes King of Kings.
Pam Drew,
Swan Bank Methodist Church,
Stoke on Trent

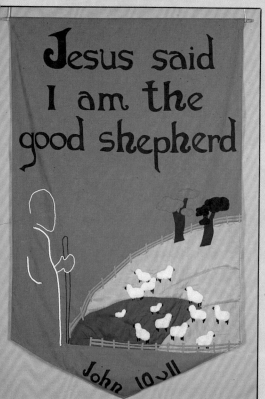

Jesus said I am the good shepherd

John 10v11

The King's Church, Chesham, Bucks

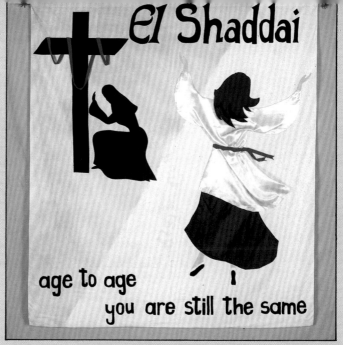

Both these banners were made to accompany dances.
The King's Church, Chesham, Bucks

The King's Church, Chesham, Bucks

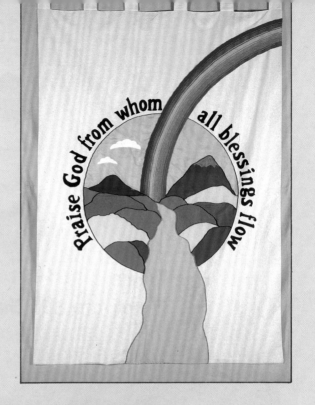

*St Mary's,
Watford, Herts*

*Cornton Baptist Church,
Stirling, Scotland*

In all your ways acknowledge Him and He will make your paths straight

The King's Church,
Amersham, Bucks

Do you love me?

Emmanuel Church,
Northwood, Middx.

The Amersham banner group 1988. From left to right:
Renee, Priscilla, Megan, Myra and Liz. Philippa was absent.

As one of the leaders, I 'knew' we could do it as a team. However, I must confess to feeling somewhat overwhelmed by it all on Tuesday 1st September, 1987. I just turned to the Bible; I found comfort in Jeremiah 8:18: 'O my Comforter in sorrow, my heart is faint within me.' Then came verses offering confidence from Hebrews 4:15–16: 'For we do not have a high priest who is unable to sympathise with our weaknesses, but we have one who has been tempted in every way—yet was without sin. Let us then approach the throne of grace with confidence....' I believed and claimed His promises. One of God's final blessings was in my quiet time on Friday 22nd April, Psalm 20:5: 'We will shout for joy when you are victorious and will lift up our banners in the Name of our God.'

My heart was overwhelmed, as it was when Les, Dorothy, Stewart and I had put everything in place at Caister on Wednesday 27th April 1988. It was a glimpse of heaven, especially as Dorothy and I sat in one of the top rows of seats in the main marquee and looked at our four large banners and the AEA one which Dorothy and Stewart had made. The tent contractors tested the lights on stage and the images came to life. It was a wonderful and fantastic experience. We really felt that God was blessing us—good measure pressed down and overflowing. We could not stay to the Celebration but left Caister at 7.40 pm and arrived home at 1.00 am—not quite on wings but truly upheld.

If you would like a full account of this project please write to 'Christian Banners' and send £1.

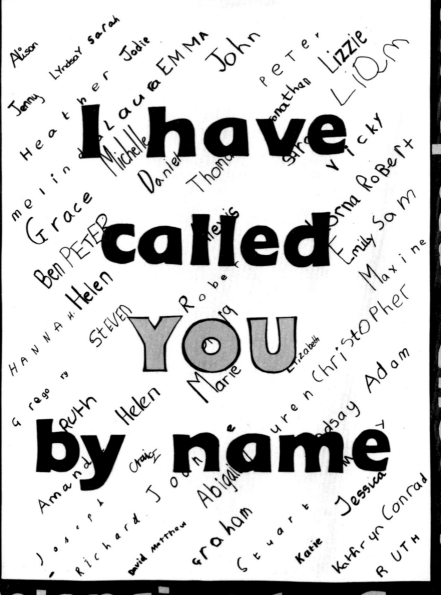

For to us a child is born
to us a son is given and
the government will
be on his shoulders.
And he will be called
Wonderful Counsellor, Mighty God
Everlasting Father, Prince of Peace.
Isaiah 9:6

Paper Sculpture

Pam Drew, Swan Bank Methodist Church,
Stoke-on-Trent

The idea of making pictures and mounting them on a church wall was one which appealed to me as a teenager. It was dismissed as a passing whim—no one ever put pictures on a church wall! The idea lay dormant for at least fifteen years until I attended a concert given by Adrian Snell in 1980.

A vivid picture was painted in my mind's eye: a silhouette of Bethlehem, made out of black boxes against a changing sky of red, orange and yellow. Thick, textured acrylic paint was daubed on four large sheets of card with a variety of brushes, sponges and cloths. These backgrounds contrasted sharply with the smooth black sugar paper which was cut into the shapes of wise men, Mary, shepherds; it was also folded to make black box shaped buildings overlaying each other to give depth and distance to Bethlehem. Scored gold card represented the light that had come into the world and formed a halo above Bethlehem. Above the four sections of this panorama soared angels made of layered white paper by using pleating, curling and cutting techniques.

How amazing it seems now to read that, at this same time, 1979–80, the Lord was also at work in many other parts of the country leading believers to raise banners to glorify Jesus.

I work within the framework of the four main festivals, Christmas, Easter, Pentecost and Harvest. They are times rich in symbolism for which there seems an endless supply of inspiration through Scriptures. As each festival time approaches, I am aware of the need to start thinking of a new design and I spend time looking through passages of Scripture which are relevant, having first prayed that the Lord would open my mind, bless my thoughts and reveal the pictorial message He has for me and the rest of our fellow-ship.

Since 1982, a permanent eight foot square board has been fixed to one of the side walls of the church and painted matt black. Staples have now replaced Blue-Tac and flat shapes are given a third dimension by being raised from the background and secured in place. Card structures can be hung away from the wall. Spotlights, which were already fixed above the board, can be angled to pick out gold and silver paper to startling effect.

The Lord has sometimes used the medium of music to inspire me. Our home is rarely quiet because I'm married to a musician and once, while he was rehearsing with a friend, 'When I survey the Wondrous Cross', the words were repeated over and over. Again a picture came to mind, which was a visual reflection of the verses: What a moving composition that hymn makes in pictorial form! I say that with no sense of pride, for it is the Lord who inspires. The difficulty I have is in offering the design—is it worthy to be described as an inspired work? Is it good enough to display as an aid to worship?

The Lord seems to like symbols. The circle was the basic shape of the 'Wondrous Cross' design representing the world. It was held up by a pair of human hands—an expression of the words 'were the whole realm of nature mine, that were an offering far too small'. The lower semi-circle was edged with a crown of thorns made from folded gold foil bent at sharp angles and a river of blood flowed from Calvary's hill and dripped in large tear shapes off the lower edge of the crown of thorns. These last two pictures portrayed the verse perhaps unmatched in the history of hymnody:

See from His head, His hands, His feet;
Sorrow and love flow mingled down
Did ere such love and sorrow meet
Or thorns compose so rich a crown.'

Additional ideas to those contained within the hymn completed the design: clouds above the empty black cross

John Ward

(painted balsa wood, backed with golden beams) represented the coming of the Son of Man in a cloud with power and great glory, Luke 21:27. Sheep and fig leaves edging the upper semi-circle, illustrated the prophecy made in Isaiah 53:7 and the parable of the fig tree, Luke 21.

Pam recommends, *Paper into Sculpture*, by Bruce Angrave. Warne's Art and Craft Series.

If you would like more information about this subject write to, Pam Drew, c/o Saltbox Christian Resource Centre, 5 Moorland Road, Burslem, Stoke-on-Trent ST6 1DJ.

Soar Like the Eagle

Naomi Lidwell, St Silas Church, Glasgow

The idea and words for this banner came to me during a time of difficulty. I meditated on them over four years before making the banner.

For the baby eaglet peering over the edge of the nest the sky seems a frightening place; but eventually he jumps and drops before his wings open and the wind takes him up. He learns that there are moments of falling, when he seems abandoned to the air, and then comes that glorious upward movement as the wind takes him high.

Reaching for the plans and fulfilment that God has for us, we can get there only by trusting Him and launching out. Jeremiah 29:11 in the Good News Bible says, 'I alone know the plans I have for you; and the Revised Standard Version continues, 'plans for good and not for evil to give you a future and a hope.'

When everything seemed a disaster and plans went into reverse I had to go to God and trust Him for the future. In so doing I found inner security, deliverance from fear and the ability to face each situation as it came. The eagle drops down only to fly even higher. We shall have ups and downs but 'those who hope in the Lord will renew their strength. They will soar on wings like eagles' (Is 40:31).

> Fed on the Father's food
> The fledgling birds will fly,
> Soaring above
> Valleys of danger and death
> Safe with the impulse of strong life within
> Maturing in the glory of motion,
> Urged on by force invisible.
> *Ruth Wood.*

For I know the plans I have for you.... Jer. 29 v 11

"trust me"

Banner-Making With Children

Yvonne Davis, Chalfont St Giles Christian Fellowship

It is my opinion that making banners with children is exhausting, exhilarating, challenging and very satisfying, probably in that order! I have often been asked by Sunday Schools, playgroups etc. to help make a frieze or similar decoration for an event, and have suggested that we make a banner instead, which is more lasting and which can be re-used.

The golden rules are: planning and preparation; many adult helpers, as much as one adult to two children with the under fives.

Children can create their own designs, given a theme and, sometimes, pictures or photos to spark them off. I never design banners for adults to make and neither do I for children. Their ideas are often far freer than my own and full of joy and vitality. I also feel that simple ideas work best with good letters cut by an older person using templates.

Two ideas that I have enjoyed recently are:
- making prints with fabric paints—hands, feet, leaves etc.
- Drawing with fabric crayons or fabric painting felt pens on material, and applying the pictures to a background with adhesive.

Both these techniques allow for real personal creativity and diversity and are different from the basic collage approach. Felt is easily cut into shapes and crimplene type fabric is also useful because it does not fray.

A banner made by
Aileen, aged 10 years old

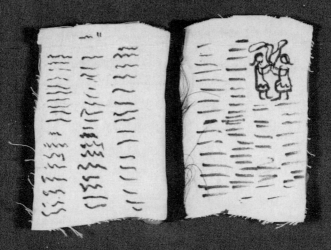

I have collected some junior craft books to give me guidelines as to what is appropriate for various age groups and what will spark off new ideas. Often children's designs, though lacking in draughtsmanship, are full of imagination. The role of the group leader is to direct it and co-ordinate the proceedings! I have often felt exhausted at the end of a children's banner-making session, but have stood back and been amazed by what has been achieved.

A picture with words inside
—an aid to picture-receiving.

Working With Children

Naomi Lidwell, St Silas Church, Glasgow

*O*ur aim is to encourage —always see something positive in each child.

Rough Outline For Workshop

- *Theme* 'Jesus is'...my Saviour, Shepherd, Friend, Light, Healer, Way, Life, Truth.
- *Worship* if possible led by themselves.
- Get them to concentrate on *one idea* and ask the Holy Spirit to give each one a picture.
- *Be still* and listen.

Aids To Picture Receiving

- Pictures with words inside, eg. shepherd—draw a sheep; inside, write adjectives and words describing a sheep.
- Have objects: eg. a candle or a lamp—to feel and examine.
- Slides of possible ideas such as different types of roads, rough, steep, smooth.

Practical Tips

Use one medium eg: paper or fabric. You can already have prepared material backgrounds from which they can choose. Make them about one or two foot in size so they can hang them at home. It might be easier to have letter templates cut out as this takes ages! This approach is a way to introduce banners into a church for the first time as people will readily accept what the children have produced.

Holiday Club Banner

Carol Clarke, Holy Trinity, Knaphill, Woking

We *have made* only one banner with children at a holiday club. The banner was called, 'Love one another'. The lettering was deliberately made a little uneven and childlike.

A number of paper templates were made (one for each child) of boys and girls, and a selection of pre-cut small squares of material, with wool scraps, lace, milk-bottle tops and fur-fabric provided.

The children chose a paper figure (in all cases a boy for a boy and a girl for a girl!). They stuck material on to the paper shapes and it was very amusing to see the boys being very creative, giving their figures red fur-fabric 'punk' hair styles and milk-bottle top decorations, whilst the girls ignored the pretty floral materials I thought they'd choose and dressed their figures in plain materials with lace glued on here and there.

Every figure was added to the banner in three rows, boys linking hands with girls throughout. The children whose age range was about 5–10 years, were thrilled to have their banner hanging in church for many months.

Banner-Making With Teenagers

Yvonne Davis

This is the one no-one wants to do! Yet, with imagination and buckets full of encouragement, teenagers have very succinct ways of expressing themselves. I have found myself being intensely moved by the passion of teenagers and have been inspired in my spiritual walk by them. This is not to say that a firm hand is not required, as well as good vocal chords!

The pre-making stage is vital. Some sort of discussion, slide-show, forum is needed to set the scene. Talking the project through and coming up with design sketches can be laborious, but always pays off. The instant answer is rarely the best, and, in this instant age, banner-making can take some putting across—have patience and determination here!

A great discovery for me has been spray paint!! Teenagers, whether secretly or openly, quite often like the 'subversive feel' of spraying with cans of paint. This realisation has greatly aided me in getting a project going, when I worked with inner-city kids, as well as with 'well churched' young people!

Calico is the best background material. The final design is chalked on and after plenty of practice, spraying can take place. Needless to say many plastic groundsheets are required.

The rules are heavily laid down concerning the handling of paint and I have not had an accident yet—even working in Salisbury cathedral! To get a good effect the spray jet has to be close to the fabric as proximity minimises the mess.

We have used car spray paint but other spray paints are available from DIY stores. The banners dry in approximately one hour and are then ready to be hung or used in a procession.

a dull scruffy
hall enhanced
by a banner

John Ward

Leading A Group

Various Contributors

This chapter is a result of group discussion. Not all groups have leaders; some meet in a less structured way and make banners for special projects, working well together with no appointed leader. Others have someone with a clearly defined role. Some would simply have a person to co-ordinate.

The leader is the person who has the vision for the banner ministry and administers and calls the dates.

The Role Of The Leader

- Encourager—helps others discover their gifts.
- Catylyst—is a channel of the Holy Spirit to others.
- Director—sets deadlines well before the date.
- Lets go his/her own interests and lets others create.
- Develops other people's gifts and recognises their skills. Doesn't let people get boxed in with the same job everytime.
- Is pastorally responsible—cares for others as people—supports them in prayer and in their lives—shares the burdens of others.
- Adjusts and improves the project stage by stage so that it grows to completion.
- Refuses ideas that are not acceptable but sees that all members have a worthwhile part to play.
- Guides the conversation away from negative thinking, grumbling and criticism.
- Helps everyone to see the potential in the others for creativity, and as the people we can become in Christ, believing and desiring the best of and for each other.

The law of the Lord is perfect,
reviving the soul.
The statutes of the Lord are trustworthy,
making wise the simple.
The precepts of the Lord are right,
giving joy to the heart.
The commands of the Lord are radiant,
giving light to the eyes.
The fear of the Lord is pure,
enduring for ever.
The ordinances of the Lord are sure and
altogether righteous.
They are more precious than gold,
than much pure gold;
they are sweeter than honey,
than honey from the comb.
By them is your servant warned;
in keeping them there is great reward.

Psalm 19:7–11

Working Together

Various Contributors

For some weeks each member of the group brought a very brief verse or thought to share (not necessarily related to banners). We went round in turn and spoke out these words. No one was allowed to interrupt or discuss. We shared something that we had gained by listening to the Lord during the previous week and so encouraged and blessed each other. The leader must keep this time brief. It is an excellent way to encourage one another to listen to the Lord.

I desire to lift up the Name of Jesus at every meeting.

Although we are a diverse and mixed group, some of us having very little artistic skill (I myself am hopeless at drawing) each one has something of value to offer and all feel they have played a part when the finished product is on view.

We need spaces in making banners. We need to accept times when nothing is happening as an opportunity to do other things or have times of quiet and contemplation. Our banner group has an idea for a patchwork banner of nine squares of the fruits of the Spirit. We could create these squares at home in the next few weeks; we would be free from the pressure of a group and have more time for our families.

Sometimes I make a cup of tea and sit down in comfort with some sewing or embroidery or knitting and relax in the presence of the Lord as my hands are busy with something I enjoy.

I ask the Lord for guidance for each meeting before people arrive to bring a Scripture or experience to the group.

Working Alone
And With Others

Priscilla Nunnerley

From time to time, I have made a banner on my own, when there were words that came to me very clearly. 'My peace I give you' was in my heart for two years before I had the space in my life to make it. I desired to know more of the peace that Jesus wants to give us.

I saw the words in white on an aquamarine background with some sort of sea scene below with rough waves and lots of subtle colours. Handling rich-coloured lamé fabrics inspired me to design a contemporary scene of a little boat in a storm with the words above, speaking dramatically into the situation.

I enjoyed experimenting with fabrics in a way I couldn't have done had it been a group project. I handstitched ruckled pieces of jade, silver and purple lamé and used sequin waste, net and white fringing to get the foam effect. The finished picture was nearly six foot in length, took 36 hours over 5 weeks and was made on a table in my spare bedroom!

It was a good experience but solitary; I feel there is a richness in a project created by a group that cannot be matched by work that is done individually.

Recently, our group allowed me to lead them in making an Easter banner from an idea of colour and design that was almost exploding inside me to get out. I think that, although leading a banner group is largely about encouraging others to have the ideas, there is a place now and again for one person to give a strong lead, buy the fabrics and direct the design to see his/her particular vision fulfilled.

Am I Hearing God?

Priscilla Nunnerley with Ruth Wood,
The King's Church, Amersham

The Lord delights to speak. He promised us His Holy
Spirit to guide us into all truth. The big question is, 'Am I
hearing from Him?'—How do I know when He wants me to
do something?

Hearing From Him On My Own

I believe the Lord has a way of letting us know what He
wants us to do. One June evening in 1988, in a Dorset country lane, I was telling a trusted friend, 'Harry', about my
uncertainty concerning another book, but of my desire to do
it. She said, 'The Lord wants us to be simple about things
and if you think He wants you to do it, go ahead and He will
stop you if it's not His will!' That was a moment of revelation
and decision and I went steadily ahead from that day.

On the subject of banners we also need to be simple.
There are many banners such as those made quickly for the
church, for processions, for small gifts, that do not need the
thought and prayer that is given to the more weighty and
magnificent creations! Many times I have just got on and
made a banner with words from the Word of God because I
wanted to do so.

Other banners are made from a word or picture that has
spoken to you deeply. Such can speak very significantly to
others. If you have any doubt about an idea put it aside and
see if the idea returns. Or ask others in your church for their
comments. Abstract pictures or very unusual images may be
suitable for a home or art gallery but not in a place of
worship.

If you are puzzled as to whether a picture or vision is
from the Lord ask yourself, 'What does this say?' If your

picture gives you a thought that is echoed in the Word of God then it is something to share and perhaps could be made into a banner.

If a design has a clear meaning you could add to the richness of the banner by choosing words that are not immediately obvious. This will stimulate further thought. See 'Such Love' (colour photo).

Hearing From Him With Others

Again, many banners will be straightforward. You do not need a long discussion on 'Praise the Lord' except perhaps on the practical details!! Illustrations from His Word of proclamation, praise and promise which are constant and universal statements are appropriate at any time of year.

Other banners require special thought. In recent years, banner groups have become increasingly aware of their role in seeking the Lord for a word that is on His heart for the people. We have desired to capture His love, might and majesty and to receive a message from Him from the Word of God that will direct us ahead—a 'now' word that speaks to a specific group of people.

There are different ways of finding this word. You must choose the most appropriate:

- People bring words they have been thinking about.
- The group meditates on the Word during a time of quiet.
- The group has a Bible study.
- Others in the church contribute ideas.
- Relevant objects or music are used to stimulate thought.
- A certain banner group usually sketches ideas on paper and then puts them all out on the table to consider. They often find a common theme coming through. If, on the odd occasion someone disagrees, they pray and rethink the design.

When the group has a sense of rightness about certain words then those are the ones. The knowledge is an inner witness to the Holy Spirit speaking. You can sense Him, but He is like the wind and you can't predict or direct Him.

If there is any question or doubt, ask the Holy Spirit's confirmation, maybe by seeking your pastor's advice. One group, on meeting to make a Christmas banner, could not decide on anything and so felt the Lord wanted them to have more time for other things at that busy season.

Our aim is to hear from God for our banners so that others may listen to Him as they look at them. A young man told the pastor that he wanted to become a Christian and, when asked what it was that spoke to him, said that it was an Easter banner, 'Behold I am alive for evermore'.

A simple design is often very much more effective than a cluttered fussy one. The impact of the design must be immediate.

Rachel McHugh

Instant Banners

Alec T. Rolls, Methodist Youth Training Officer

A five minute introduction to banner making proved sufficient to motivate and guide young and old in Banner Making during Ecumenical Workshops and Worship Days in Devon.

The banners completed in just over an hour by the workshop participants were then displayed later that day during an Act of Celebration in worship. Some fifteen brightly coloured banners proclaimed the Good News of Easter and Pentecost and brought a new dimension to the worship.

The method used was by means of an overhead project or (see page 84) which enlarged outline drawings traced from the Good News Bible and other sources on to the transparency and then projected them on to large sheets of paper. The outlines were then cut out and used as templates. Hessian or other cloth, dowel rod, felt and material and scissors were provided or brought by participants.

Folks were so excited at having created something beautiful and artistic which they could be really proud of as a contribution to worship and then take home to display in their own Churches.

Another idea for instant banners is to give groups of 3/4 people, scissors, glue and 3 blending colours of card eg purple, gold and pale blue, and ask them to choose 1, 2 or 3 words and a design which those colours suggest.

Fabrics

Yvonne Davis

As a child there was nothing I liked more than to rummage through my mother's scrap bag. I have to admit to the same delight still! Scraps are essential to banner-makers, because you often do not know what you will need until the last moment.

The background cloth is very important as it sets the tone of the banner. Cheap stretchy material as a background can ruin the project. I tend to buy firm cloth as the main investment. Fabrics such as corduroy, denim, calico, drill, velvet etc. make excellent backcloths but lighter fabrics such as polycotton, silk etc. can be used and sometimes interlined.

The actual basics of squaring up the backing piece of material can be quite difficult. Often the weave isn't straight so one cannot just pull a thread. Although there is a great temptation to rush ahead it is wise to take time to get this first stage right.

Someone else has commented, 'It is important to have a good weight, close-weave fabric for the backing! Apart from that ruling we break all the rules and mix silks, wools, fur fabrics, felts on a banner. A firm backing allows you to do this.'

Felt is very useful for lettering, is wonderful for cutting intricate shapes and has a good range of colours. Other fabrics can be obtained by requests in the church bulletin and at jumble sales. Crimplene and PVC are useful because of their non-fray properties.

Very frayable cloths like lurex and lamé can be stiffened by ironing fine vilene to the back. This technique can also work on materials like japsilk and chiffon. Quite a variety of fabrics can be used for largish lettering if first backed with iron-on vilene.

Net can be used to give beautiful effects of water or sky. Several thicknesses create rich colours and ruckled-up white net can create a waterfall. Net needs to be sewn with invisible thread for best effect.

We keep colours in colour-coded bags so that all sorts of texture-colour combinations can be easily found. This variety aids design and can add wonderful interest by stimulating new ideas.

I think there is a place sometimes for real extravagance of beautiful fabrics, wonderful colours, net, beads, cord and perhaps embroidery. We can praise God and thank Him and celebrate His love by an exuberant, enthusiastic, joyful response.

However other themes will require quieter colours and more formal letters—and some like the one of the prison cell—very sombre colours.

Most of us making banners are given the cost of the materials by our churches. The amount is modest compared with most other expenses.

Read about the directions the Lord gave for wonderful materials for the tabernacle and temple in Exodus—chapters 26–40 and II Chronicles–chapters 2–7.

Priscilla Nunnerley

Colour

Evelyn Lucas, The King's Church, Amersham

An Awareness Of Colour

Colour can affect the viewer for good and be a form of therapy but it can have an adverse effect. While a large area of bright, intense garish colour may give the impression of happiness to most people it may disturb a few. Similarly, a drab banner can have a very negative effect. These colours may suit the theme of the banner but the result may be very different from that intended.

Colour Relationships

Consult one of the many art and needlework books with a colour section. Experiment by placing a green square on a larger magenta square and then place the green square on a different green. You will see that the two opposing colours appear bright and intense while the two similar colours seem to cancel one another out.

Sometimes it is pleasing to use different shades of the same colour but it can also produce dull results. A small amount of red close to the centre of focus can often bring such a banner to life and draw the viewer to the focal point. Try to decide in the planning stage where your centre of focus is going to be. Everything else should be subservient to this decision—don't overdo it but be aware of it.

The Choice Of Colours

Colour can be used to create a 3D effect. Things receding into the background are affected by the atmosphere and will appear to be a different colour. Hills will appear blue/grey from a distance. Use this knowledge to create depth.

Use a soft background and a stronger colour for letters; but if the picture is to tell the story then reduce the colour in the words. Perhaps hold a session where you just look at colours and experiment with them or invite an artist to talk about the subject.

Experiences Of Colour

Many public buildings such as social security offices, housing departments, hospitals and law courts have a stark coldness—a feeling of a power structure that can seem uncaring and unloving. Somehow you have to win through despite the surroundings. In some churches today the same starkness prevails.

Churches with bright banners, telling of God's love and care in Christ's death, make me feel so different. I don't need to struggle because the banner conveys the fact that the battle has been won already. So a banner in lovely colours can lift my spirit and bring me warmth and joy.

Yvonne Brooks

My mother told me that I always used to love picking colourful flowers as a small child. Perhaps this preference was a reflection of the fact that wartime produced little colour. In later years, when I suffered periods of darkness, I sometimes saw flowers at unexpected moments, as when I perceived a beautiful orange-red rose in the rain, through a window.

Working on the banners for my new church has given me a sense of responsibility, and the Lord has used my natural eye for colour to create banners, which provide an attractive focal point that stands out from the gold leaf which is predominant in the Gold Room, which is hired out to us every Sunday morning for worship.

Wendy Toller

Colour creates the mood—atmosphere, light, darkness, warmth, cold, friction and conflict and Majesty. There are no set rules regarding the use of colour in banner making but the too liberal use of colour can destroy the impact of what could be a purposeful banner.

George Holden

Wonderful colour effect of this banner by Katherine Keast. Joshua is magenta and Caleb golden yellow against the black background.

Designing

Clare Ashburner, The King's Church, Amersham

$O_{nce\ the\ words}$ and the concept are confirmed by the Holy Spirit, it is time to design. It is important not to hurry this stage, as time spent perfecting the design will reap benefits in the excellence of the finished banner. It would be senseless to spend valuable time making up a banner that was a failure because insufficient time had been taken at the design stage.

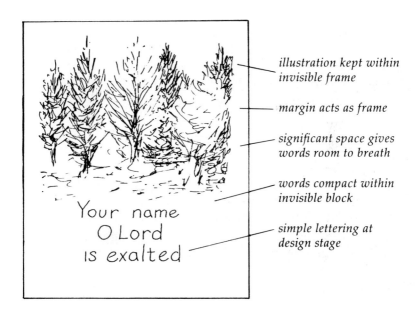

— illustration kept within invisible frame

— margin acts as frame

— significant space gives words room to breath

— words compact within invisible block

— simple lettering at design stage

Your name
O Lord
is exalted

Aim to be beautiful, whatever is lovely, think about such things.

BE CLEAR   Don't overload the design with 'significant' ideas.

BE SIMPLE   Beauty is the absence of superfluity.

BE SUBTLE   Don't feel bound to state the obvious but leave the observers' mind room to fill in the gaps.

Take a large sheet of paper and a soft pencil—3-6B—and start doodling. This is not to show whether or not you can draw, but to prove to yourselves that you have thought about what you are planning and have considered alternatives.

Play around with ideas, and don't confine yourself to accepting the first idea that comes to mind. Imagine new ways of seeing your concept, and roughly sketch them out, remembering that this is not the time to go into great detail. This is a good opportunity for inspiration which you may well be given.

Consider your commission; is there a best size and shape for the spot where the banner is to hang? Measure and draw four or more small rectangles (5 x 7 cm) or appropriate shapes roughly to scale and place your various ideas in them.

The words must be incorporated at this stage as part of the balanced design. As the words are important let them stand out well by the significance of the space they are given, not just by their size. This is the easiest time to make improvements.

Now choose your best design or draw another rectangle and incorporate the best ideas. Finally you can go on to a more detailed drawing in an enlarged version.

Remember that banners with life-giving words, excellently designed and worked, will always be a blessing.

Considering different
approaches to the subject.

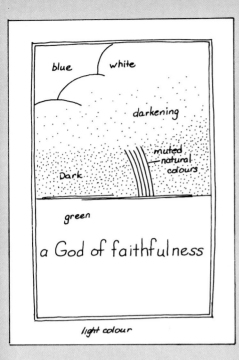

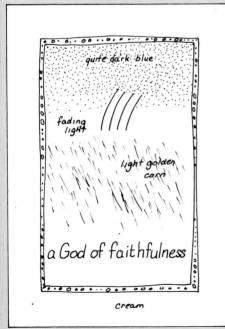

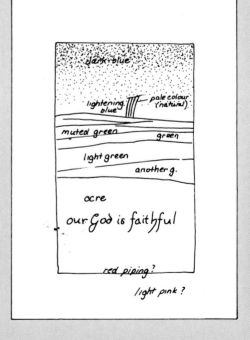

Lettering

Clare Ashburner

Through the media we are very accustomed to reading excellently designed lettering. As the words on our banners are important, there is also a need for excellence, though many banners slip at this point. Here are some guidelines for success!

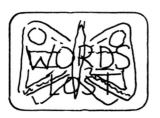

Lettering should be seen as an integral part of the design, not added as an after thought in the largest available space. It needs a real place of its own where it has room to breath.

The letters must be the right size in relation to the banner design.

They should be of a coherent style in keeping with their message or mood.

Spacing is vitally important. As a general rule keep the letters as close together as possible without actually crowding them.

Make sure that the 'weight' of the letters is consistent.

Lower case letters are always easier to read THAN UPPER CASE WHEN THERE ARE SEVERAL WORDS TOGETHER.

I
D
E
A
PU*ZZLES*
F
O
R

Words placed horizontally are more comfortable to read than vertical ones.

The message of the words often comes across better when the words follow on from each other rather than being spread across a design in ones and twos.

Use a grid of lines to get the right proportional size for individual letters.

Often the drafting of the letters is not done until the banner is well advanced. As long as the designed space is still there, this is quite in order. At this stage, rectangles of paper roughly proportionate to the letter size (narrower for 'i' wider for 'w') can be laid on the banner to ascertain the actual size needed before each letter is drawn.

Learn the basic disciplines for lettering from books on calligraphy. One member of a group might feel led to make a special study of lettering design, collecting illustrations and examples, though all hands are needed to make and sew!

Always get someone else to check the spelling!

Enlarging Figures And Lettering

Philippa Soundy, The King's Church, Amersham

Introduction

We produced a banner for Christmas, 1987, depicting Mary and the boy Jesus, with the verse, 'The Word became flesh and lived for a while among us'. (See colour photographs) Since time was short and none of us great artists, we used two techniques to help us make the banner.

Enlargement Of Figures

We wanted to show Mary seated, and Jesus as a boy of about six years, and found some figures in the Good News Bible which, with slight modifications, would be just right. We drew the figures (as we wanted them to appear) on an acetate sheet, and then used an overhead projector to project them onto a large piece of paper (ideally it should be thin card) held against a wall. We drew around the outlines on the projected figures (by now about 30 inches high) and cut them out to use as templates for our chosen fabrics. The resulting figures were simple and clear.

Production Of Large-Scale Text

For the lettering, we experimented with printouts from a home computer, on a dot-matrix printer. The programme used was a very simple one, ('Sign Designer' by Software Publishing Corporation) such as many computer enthusiasts would own, capable of producing three different styles of lettering, in any size up to 8 inches high. We chose the simplest style and printed the letters about 3 inches high, within a few minutes. We then cut out the paper letters and used them as templates in the usual way.

Simple Steps
In Letter Making

Dorothy Smith, Cornton Baptist Church,
Stirling, Scotland

D*ecide prayerfully* on a style of lettering appropriate for text and picture.

Decide dimensions of letters. Rule out computer paper into rectangles of suitable size to draw letters in.

Sketch letters lightly into the rectangles, using a soft pencil so you can make adjustments (on curves, for example) easily.

Place iron-on vilene (shiny side up) on top of the computer paper and trace the letters using a sharp pencil or a roller or ball point pen. Use a ruler to ensure the straight lines are straight!

Place fabric on top of vilene and turn both over to check that the letter guide lines are clearly visible. If they are, iron fabric carefully to the vilene backing. If not, mark the lines more visibly.

Cut out letters carefully. To minimise creasing or fraying handle the letters as little as possible. Lay out a sheet of computer paper and as you cut each letter out in order, place on top of the other letters. When finished, fold the paper round the letters and keep safely in a polythene bag until they are needed to glue to the banner.

Another Group Uses Iron-on Vilene

We've found by trial and error that vilene ironed on the back of felt is an excellent help when tracing the template of the letter onto the material—remembering to trace the letter on back to front! Also, if using material other than felt, once the outline of the letter has been drawn on we've used a sewing machine on a close zigzag stitch to work round the shape before we cut it out. This method has been very successful even with loose woven material like lurex!

Hawkwell Parish Church, Essex.

Bondaweb Is Another Group's Choice*

A letter-style is chosen and then copied and enlarged by eye between two parallel lines of the desired height—we usually use letters about 4" high. The lettering is traced using Bondaweb* and a black felt tip with the rough side of the Bondaweb uppermost. The letters are then ironed face down on to the material to be used for the letters. If the lettering is a dark colour, trace with pale tailor's chalk. The outline of the letters can then be clearly seen through the Bondaweb and cut out. All that remains is to peel off the paper backing, place in position on the banner and iron on. It works best with cotton mixtures and felt.

*Bondaweb At present I have only found it in small packets containing about 2ft x 5" and it costs just under £1. I have read somewhere that it is available by the yard but I have yet to discover this. Full instructions for its use are on the packet.

Techniques

Avril Norton, Biggin Hill Christian Fellowship, Kent

Embroidery

We need to get away from the idea that embroidery is only satin and chain stitch on tablecloths. If you have not been to an exhibition of embroidery lately, I urge you to go. Look out for City and Guild Students' Assessment exhibitions at local colleges.

I, personally, have benefitted from being a member of the Embroiderers' Guild. To find your local branch contact The Embroiderers' Guild, Apartment 41A, Hampton Court Palace, East Molesey, Surrey, KT8 9AU. Their meetings and workshops have opened my eyes to numerous new techniques which can be used in banner-making. At a weekly embroidery class, too, I have also been able to share about what our group does and to show photos of our banners—a real opportunity to witness.

Many excellent books can also give us ideas and teach new techniques. Do scour your local bookshops and libraries as new books are constantly being written. Some authors I recommend are: Jan Beaney, Jan Messent, Diana Springall and Richard Box.

One important point we feel is that we should always remember that what we do is for the Lord. Our banner-making is not a means for our own artistic experiments. Our prayer and meditation are all-important. The words and design are known to God before we start. He will reveal them to us. We may incorporate new techniques and use our creative skills but only as part of an overall, God-inspired banner.

So many books explain stitch possibilities but some to consider are fly and cretan stitch for plants, grass effects, flowers etc.; straight or irregular running stitch and irregular cross stitch to fill large areas; couching, especially of thicker and textured threads for tree bark, fields, plant stalks, and for outlining.

One technique which we have used is free machine embroidery. This is really not difficult—do try. It is explained in detail in books such as: *The New Machine Embroidery*—Joy Clucal, *Machine Embroidery*—Moyra McNeill, *Thread Painting*—Liz Hubbard (explains use with paints). We have found machine embroidery useful for adding colour, texture, line and movement to plain fabric, and for sewing on small pieces of fabric, wool or textured thread.

Paints

Spray Paints   Although car aerosol spray paints have a good effect it is better to use ozone friendly spray paints or other spirit-based ones (art and craft shop). For variations in colour mix and overlap sprays with or without masking a stencil. Use sprays outside on a still day or in a well-ventilated room. Cut newspaper or card to protect all areas not to be painted.

Acrylic Paints   (eg Rowney's Cryla Colour) are water or P.V.A. soluble and are quick drying. We have used them in several ways.
- *Painting* directly onto fabric with a brush (use a good quality one). This method can be used on colour fabric, for shading, and as a base for stitchery.
- *Printing* onto fabric, using pieces of wood, cork, polystyrene, string, corrugated card rolled end on or torn to get rib effects. Experiment! The textured effects can be excellent eg: wood grain, stone walls, pebble paths etc.
- *Spraying*: make up a thin mixture of the colour required in a small bottle (we use perm lotion bottles). Use a metal mouth diffuser to blow the paint onto the banner. These come from art shops at about £1.50. Practise first onto newspaper. The effects vary depending on how hard you blow and how close to the banner you are but generally

The Sower

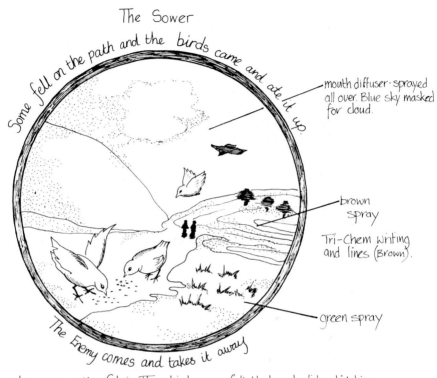

Some fell on the path and the birds came and ate it up.

mouth diffuser-sprayed all over. Blue sky masked for cloud.

brown spray

Tri-Chem writing and lines (Brown).

green spray

The Enemy comes and takes it away

Very pale green cotton fabric. Three birds - grey felt, black and white stitching. One bird, figures grass and trees - straight stiched. Seeds - yellow french knots and tiny beads. Size 20cm.

This is one part of a banner now hanging in the home of a missionary in the Far East, and prompts many conversations about the gospel.

give a more spotty effect than aerosol sprays. Do remember to take it easy and breathe in a lot of fresh air yourself!

Fabric Paints Most widely available are Dylon, Deka, Pelikan and Seta. They are all slightly different so experiment with what you can buy, being careful about mixing colour from different ranges. Most are used directly onto the fabric and then are fixed on by ironing. You need to consider whether the fabric you use will take a hot iron.

Several fabric marker pens are also available and ordinary felt pens can be used. Check to see whether they run. Fabricrayons are used to draw onto paper which is then ironed onto fabric.

Tri-Chem paints come in a wide range of colours—plain, sparkly and puff-effect. The paint is in a tube with a ball-point end and is used rather like a biro. It is very long-lasting and washable. The paints can be used to fill in large areas of colour, to add areas of shade, texture and pattern. They are particularly useful for adding fine detail (facial features, parts of flowers etc.) and for outlining and sharpening edges. As they are so versatile their use needs to be explained so they are usually obtained on a Party-Plan basis. Write, mentioning this book, to: The Tri-Chem Company International, Cherrycourt Way, Stanbridge Road, Leighton Buzzard, Bedfordshire LU7 8UH. Tel: Leighton Buzzard 379100. They will put you in touch with your local Instructor, or tell you how to purchase by post from their catalogue.

Sally Dakin. St Matthews Oxford adds *Stencilling*

Stencilling techniques work very well with big, bold, simple designs. Plain, light-coloured untreated fabric—cotton, linen etc.—makes a good background: sheets are ideal, and the machined hem may be wide enough for a (slim) hanging pole!

Any kind of paint, ink or dye can be used. It can be applied with a paintbrush, a spray bottle/atomiser (from a chemist's shop), or an aerosol can. For outdoor banners, waterproof paint will be needed: car paint/spray or permanent fabric paint are ideal.

Stencils are made by cutting the desired shape out of paper or card. For a negative stencil, the shape is then attached to the fabric and the exposed fabric around the shape is covered with paint. When the shape is removed the area beneath is still the original colour of the fabric. For a positive stencil, the piece of paper or card from which the shape was cut is attached to the fabric, and the area inside is painted, leaving the rest of the fabric the original colour.

Other Techniques

If you refer to, *Banners in His Name,* you will find short chapters on spray-paint, batik and torn-paper collage. The banner books are unable to provide full details of techniques but there are many specialized books available. Take courage and experiment and you will be surprised at the results!

Love is patient
Love is Kind
Love rejoices with the truth
It always protects
    always trusts
    always hopes
    always perseveres
Love never fails

A wedding banner
with cord lettering
and silk flowers.
Burgess Hill,
Baptist Church
West Sussex

Share The Lord Through Banners

Rachel McHugh, St Mary's, Harrogate

Banner Evenings. Invite another banner group and enjoy an informal time.

Banner Days. Invite 3 or 4 other churches and arrange a talk and some practical workshops.

Displays. Exhibit by hiring a local hall or at a craft fair.

Writing. Write an accompanying leaflet for a series of banners or for the church magazine or a book. More are needed.

Talking. Visit another church to give a talk to potential banner-makers or a wider audience. Seek for opportunities rather than wait for them to happen.

Using banners for special occasions when many visitors are present—weddings—baptisms—funerals.

Borrow. If banners are needed for a special event, consider borrowing from another church or borrow sometimes just to add variety.

Library. A group of churches in an area could compile a list of their banners with details, including a contact phone number for each church so that banners could be borrowed directly.

Photograph Album. Keep a record to show others.

Overseas. Give banners to friends overseas, if possible with the appropriate language.

Sources

'Christian Banners' is a registered charity and covers only the sale of the books. It does not supply materials.

Since Tiberias Crafts closed we have not found another comprehensive source of supply but suggest you take opportunities to search out some suitable shops when travelling further afield. Look in the yellow pages under Arts and Crafts—Visit John Lewis and other big stores—Local markets—Asian markets—Jumble sales. Ask friends for unwanted silks, materials, necklaces, plain curtains.

Borovick Fabrics is an Aladdin's cave of 1,000s of fabrics supplied for fashion, stage, screen and T.V. and church needlework. They only supply fabrics. There is no catalogue but write, with specific details of the type of fabric, colour and use sending a S.A.E. They will send samples with prices and widths. Then you order sending the payment. S. Borovick, 16 Berwick Street, London W1. 01 437 2180/0520.

Whaleys (Bradford) Ltd supply silks, cotton, silk and other materials for dyeing and printing, calico, canvas, linen, wadding etc. Send stamp for catalogue to Whaleys (Bradford) Ltd, Harris Court, Great Horton, Bradford, West Yorkshire, BD7 4EQ. Tel: 0274 576718

Mini Prints produce photos from your colour negatives and prints, which you can mount on greeting cards. Various sizes—from 25 prints upwards. Mini Prints Ltd, Knowle Green, Longridge, Preston PR3 2YN Lancs. Helpful on the telephone. 0254 878878.

Seeds. Is a Christian creative resource service which will help you develop skills and talents within your church to help you apply the God-given gift of the imagination to worship. Seeds take workshops in creativity, in worship, the performing arts, music, visual arts, writing, communication skills and video. Write to 'Seeds', c/o Ingrebourne, 51 Pole Barn Lane, Frinton-on-sea, Essex, CO13 9NQ.

Paul Alexander of 'Seeds' has a book, 'Creativity in Worship' being published by Darton, Longman and Todd in March 1990, available in bookshops.

Recommended Books

Letraset catalogue. A book of alphabets in different styles, obtainable from art or graphic shops. *Chartpak* is another book of instant lettering which will give you different designs.

The Calligraphy Source Book compiled by Miriam Stribley, published by Macdonald and Co, £9.95. An attractive and useful book on this type of lettering. *The Banner Book* by Betty Wolfe—Morehouse-Barlow & Co, Inc. Wilton, Connecticut has been in and out of print twice and is at present out of print. It is very helpful if you can secure a copy.

Help I Can't Draw? Three books published by Falcon.

I Can't Draw But by Yvonne Davis (who contributed to this book). Half the book is about starting banner making. £1.20 includes postage from Seeds (see sources for address).

Picture It by Paul Clowney. Bible Society. Ideas for visual art in a church; only a little about banners.

Appliqué. Evangeline Shears and Diantha Fielding. Pan Craft Books.

Culture in a Christian Perspective—Leland Ryken. £8.95 Multnomah Press. UK agents, Scripture Press, Raans Road, Amersham, Bucks.

The Crafts Council information centre is open to the public from 10–5, Tues–Fri. Information available includes: lists of short leisure courses, craft fairs, craft guilds and societies, suppliers of material and equipment. Write for information stating exact requirements and enclosing a stamped addressed label, Craft Council, 12 Waterloo Place, London SW1 4AU. 01 930 4811.

To God be the glory